MW00873092

THE NEW

Minibeasts EDITION

...ebbie Opat

word from our editor

...NIBEASTS are tiny crea-
...es that can be found almost
...erywhere—on land, in the
...und, in the air and in the
...

Minibeasts are creatures
...t do not have backbones.
...me have hard shells, and
...ers are soft, like slugs.
...ere are over a million dif-
...ent types living on our
...rth.

Have you ever wondered
...v minibeasts can survive

among people and animals
that tower over them? Find out
about these tiny creatures in
this edition of *The News*.

Daily sp●t

Minibeasts inspire musicians!
Adam Ant was a famous
singer. Other bands are Iron
Butterfly, the Beatles, Insect
Surfers, Halo of Flies and
Sting. Isn't that a buzz?

Minibeasts

Built to survive in extraordinary conditions.

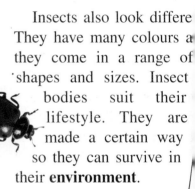

MINIBEASTS are all built differently to suit their way of life. This means they are better at some things than others.

Let's look at insects. Their bodies have three sections: head, **thorax** (say *thor-aks*) and **abdomen** (say *ab-doh-men*).

The head has the eyes, **antennae** (say *an-ten-ay*) and mouth. The thorax is where the wings and legs are. The abdomen is at the tail end of the creature. The abdomen has important body parts that insects use to eat and breathe.

Even though all insects have the same three body parts, it does not mean they are all the same. Some insects have bigger wings than others. Their legs and mouths can be different too. Some legs are for jumping. Others are for running or crawling, digging or swimming. Some insect mouths are for chewing, others are used for sucking.

Insects also look differe They have many colours a they come in a range of shapes and sizes. Insect bodies suit their lifestyle. They are made a certain way so they can survive in their **environment**.

Make sense of this!

sect minibeasts rely on their senses.

NSECTS USE their senses to find food and to find a ate. They also use their es, ears, noses and mouths protect themselves from emies.

Insects have compound es. These eyes are made up thousands of small, six-led eyes. This means insects n see in all directions without moving their heads.

Many insects use their antennae to hear. Others use the vibrations on the earth to hear noises around them.

An ant uses its legs to feel the vibrations on the ground. A lacewing (an insect with delicate wings) picks up sound through its wings. Crickets' ears are in their legs just below their knees!

A lot of insects sleep in the daytime and stay up all night. These insects do not rely on their eyes because it is often too dark to see. Instead, their bodies make a special odour which other insects can smell with their antennae.

Insects also use their antennae to taste and feel.

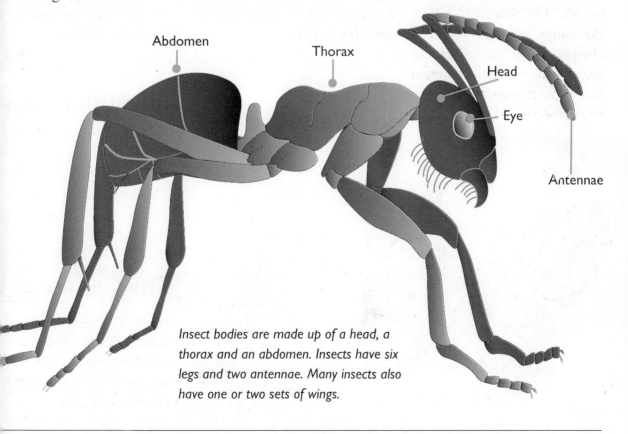

Abdomen   Thorax   Head   Eye   Antennae

Insect bodies are made up of a head, a thorax and an abdomen. Insects have six legs and two antennae. Many insects also have one or two sets of wings.

Level-headed ladybirds avoid enemies

Ladybirds are clever at keeping themselves safe.

LADYBIRDS ARE brightly coloured beetles that have black spots on their backs. Their enemies are birds and other small animals.

Ladybirds have special ways to make sure that their enemies don't come anywhere near them.

They squirt a juice from their legs that smells terrible. If the smell isn't enough to keep their enemies away, the taste is even worse!

Ladybirds have another life-saving talent. They can flip onto their backs and play dead if an enemy is nearby.

When ladybirds are not flying, the fold their wings away under their hard outer shell.

The News Cartoon

Superbugs

Ladybird girl

Cockroach Boy

Grasshopper Boy

Ant Girl

Able to Squirt horrible stuff at anyone she doesn't like.

Able to Scuttle unbelievably fast.

Able to lift 3 times her own weight

Able to leap tall buildings in a single bound!

Lawless ladybird eat aphids

LADYBIRDS can be as sm as 3 mm ($^1/_{10}$ inch) or as big 9 mm ($^3/_{10}$ inch). They have legs for crawling and a pair wings for flying.

Ladybirds eat tiny inse called **aphids** (say *ay-fid*) mites which live on plants.

So, if a ladybird is sca of birds, aphids must be afr of ladybirds.

Do you think there is teeny-weeny minibeast tha afraid of an aphid?

Fashion flash

Imagine… What if ladybirds could stage a fashion parade? Here's how it might be reported in the local ladybird magazine.

THIS SUMMER, ladybirds are wearing quite a few different outfits that look great on their lovely round bodies. Red is the most popular colour. Some are in orange, and others are in yellow. Almost all are covered in black spots.

Some ladybirds choose to be different. They decorate themselves with white or yellow spots instead of black.

Ladybird fashion is very important because it makes the enemy stay away! Their bright colours are a warning that they taste terrible.

Crazy cockroaches sleep when it's light

Then they party all night.

W HEN THE DAY comes to an end, most humans and other creatures put their heads down and sleep. But not ALL creatures sleep at night! Some like to party!

Cockroaches love to rest during the day. They find places to hide so people can't catch them. Some of their favourite hiding places are under fridges or in cracks in the walls and floors.

Cockroaches have oval, flat, greasy bodies so they can squeeze through tiny cracks. Their long antennae can sense movement, warning them of danger so they can scuttle away quickly.

Some people think that cockroaches carry diseases but this is not true. However, they can carry germs on their bodies. It depends on where they have just been.

If cockroaches have been your kitchen you will pro ably know the next morni because there will be traces the grease that is left by th bodies. It stinks!

Daily Spot

Cockroaches do not bleed red blood. When they are squashed they ooze blood that is white.

A cockroach dream

Imagine… If a cockroach could have anything in the world, this might be its dream of a perfect life.

S THE SUN comes up, cockroaches hide away to sleep all day. Snuggled under the fridge, out of the reach of nasty humans (and their VERY big shoes) a cockroach dreams of its perfect life…

In the kitchen is a feast. Breadcrumbs are scattered on the floor. Next to the fridge is a rotting apple core. After the kitchen, the cockroach gang sneak in to the bedroom.

They snack on a pair of smelly old sneakers and a dirty t-shirt under the bed.

The fun's not over yet. It's time for the cockroaches to go outside. They meet under a pile of bark, then crawl or fly to nearby bushes and eat dead leaves. They munch on tasty, rotting fruit and nibble on as many dead insects as possible before the sun rises again.

Whew! What an appetite. No wonder they spend all day sleeping it off. The perfect life for a cockroach sounds pretty yucky and smelly to me!

Daily Spot

A cockroach can live for a week without its head. It actually dies of thirst because it no longer has a mouth to drink water.

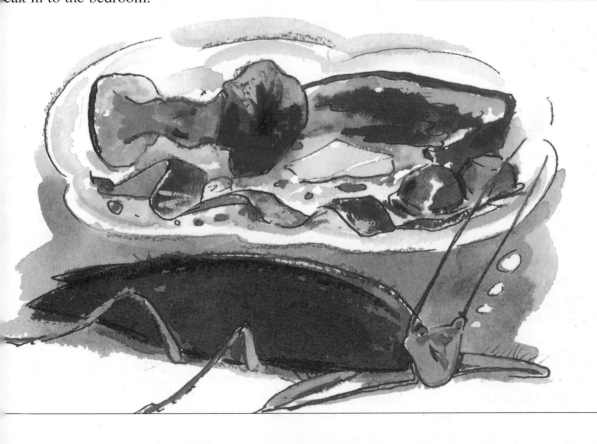

Snail trails to slime time

SNAILS ARE **gastropods** (say *gas-troh-pods*). Their feet are on their bellies. This unusual way of getting around allows snails to live in fresh water, in the ocean and on the land.

Land snails, like the ones that live in your garden, lay a track of slime to help them move about.

Snails have ribbon-like tongues with thousands of tiny teeth on them, which help to break down their food.

Snail shells have a spiral pattern. Some coil to the left, others to the right. The shell protects the snail from its enemies and also from the weather. Snails pull their bodies into their shells if they sense danger.

Most snails have eyes on the ends of long antennae. Some snails eat plan in the garden for lunch. Other types of snails end up as lunch themselves. France, they are called **escargot** *(say es-car-go).*

Is it a bird? Is it a plane?

No, it's a dragonfly.

HOW MANY times can you clap your hands in one second? Twice? Maybe three times? A dragonfly can flap its wings between twenty and thirty times in one second!

Some scientists think that dragonflies can fly at speeds of more than 100 kilometres (60 miles) per hour over short distances. Their wings are so fine, they don't look strong enough to go that fast!

Dragonflies zoom through the air backwards and forwards, up and down, doing somersaults and catching food. If an insect flies past, a dragonfly can catch it in mid-air.

They would be fabulous acrobats in the circus, don't you think?

Unlike ladybirds, dragonflies do not have a shell to hide their wings in when they are not using them. When dragonflies take a rest from all that fast flying, they spread their wings right out.

Weather

Today's weather should be warm and tropical. Watch out if you are near water. We expect many dragonflies to be flying about. This is their favourite weather.

Did you know?

One dragonfly can eat as much as its own body weight in 30 minutes.

Fact of the day

A falcon can fly even faster than a dragonfly. It hunts the dragonflies and catches them in mid-air.

First parents match then eggs do hatch

AFTER A male and female butterfly have mated, the female butterfly finds a plant to lay her eggs on. The eggs are very sticky so they don't fall off the leaves of the plant.

Inside the egg, a baby insect grows and grows. Finally the egg **hatches** and a little caterpillar crawls out. It folds the leaf it was born on and sticks it together with silk thread. The caterpillar then hides inside and eats the leaf.

It can actually eat thousands of times its own body weight in leaves. The more the caterpillar eats, the more it grows and, before long, it is too big for its old skin.

This is called **moulting**. The caterpillar grows a new skin before it gets too big for its old skin. Then, when its old skin splits open, it crawls out.

Next, the caterpillar finds a leaf stem. It makes a silk thread to help it hang from the stem. It takes a few hours to turn into a **pupa** (say *pew-pa*).

Inside the pupa, an amazing change takes place. After three weeks, the hard covering on the pupa splits open and a butterfly crawls out.

Word of the day

METAMORPHOSIS (say *met-a-mor-fa-sis*)—changing from a crawling caterpillar into a beautiful butterfly.

WANTED

My name is Bruce and I'm a male butterfly. I am looking for a lady butterfly with brightly coloured wings and a nice personality. My hobbies are flying and dancing. I would like to meet a female who wants to have babies.

The butterfly looks around for a plant to lay her eggs on.

When the eggs hatch, a caterpillar crawls out.

The caterpillar turns into a pupa and comes out as a butterfly.

Bright butterflies, marvellous moths

There are about 130,000 known species of moths around the world.

MOTHS AND butterflies are like close cousins. They have a lot in common, but they are not from exactly the same family!

Most butterflies fly during the day while most moths are seen flying around at night.

Butterflies are brightly coloured and moths are coloured to look like their surroundings.

When butterflies take a rest they lift their wings up behind their backs but moths leave their wings flat.

If you look *very* closely there is also a difference their antennae. Butterfly antennae have little knobs on their tips and moth antennae are plain.

Even though they have some differences, they have many things the same. Especially the way they grow from being an egg, into a caterpillar, and then change from a pupa into an adult moth or butterfly.

The number of different species of butterflies is about 18,000.

Fact of the day

The largest butterfly is the birdwing butterfly from New Guinea. It is 28 cm (11 inches) long. The smallest butterfly is the dwarf blue butterfly of South Africa which is just over 1 cm (less than $1/2$ inch) long.

Birth Notice

Bruce and Betty butterfly are pleased to announce that their eggs have hatched. They are now the proud parents of a group of hungry caterpillars. Mother and babies are doing well.

To bee or not to bee?

Who wants to live in a hive?

THOUSANDS OF honey bees live together in hives. These hives are like busy towns. The queen bee is in charge!

The queen bee mates with male bees called **drones**. A queen bee lives for about five years. She lays thousands of eggs during that time.

The other bees are worker bees. Worker bees feed the queen bee and look after her by licking her to keep her clean. They also take care of the young bees and fix, clean and guard the hive against wasps and other enemies.

Only females have a sting. Bees use their sting to protect their community.

Bees have barbs on the sting so it gets stuck in th skin of their enemies. Bees d after using and losing the sting.

Fact of the day

Bees talk by dancing. If they dance in a circle, it means food is nearby. Lots of tail wagging means food is far away.

Cross-section of a beehive.

A beehive has many cells made of wax.

Some cells in the hive have white wax tops. Th are full of honey.

Worker bees fill the cells with honey. The honey is made from the nectar bees have collected.

Worker bees build the hive from wax. They ma the wax inside their bodies.

The cells with yellow silk tops are the cocoons of the baby bees.

Make your own ant farm

Follow these easy steps.

T IS VERY interesting to watch an ant community in action. They may be tiny, but you could be surprised by how hard they work and how busy they all seem. Why not try to make your own ant farm so you can watch them work?

You will need:

a large glass jar
a piece of cardboard
(bigger than the opening
of the jar)
a pan
soil
ants

What to do:

1 Fill the jar with wet soil and place the jar in the pan.
2 Fill the pan with water. This acts as a moat to keep the ants from wandering away.

3 To start the farm, gather several dozen ants from a local ant nest. Try to include some ants with wings if you can, or the farm won't last very long.
4 Cut a small hole in the centre of the piece of cardboard and set it on top of the jar. Feed the ants honey, pieces of fruit, egg, or peanut butter.

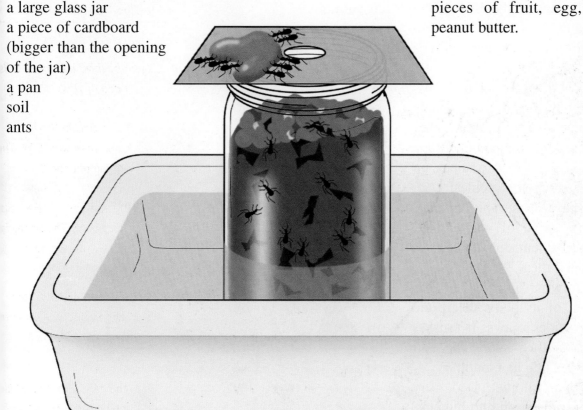

Ants are very busy creatures. You will be amazed as you watch them working in your ant farm.

Eight-year-old hero saves her father

Imagine... Last night, Mr Smith was found standing on a chair in the kitchen, screaming.

MR SMITH'S daughter, Edwina, had been learning about spiders at school. She was able to calm her father by catching the spider and showing it to him.

Edwina pointed out the eight legs of the spider. She said the legs are hairy to help them grip walls and ceilings so the spider doesn't fall off.

"This spider is female. It's body is bigger than a male spider so she can carry her eggs," Edwina explained.

"It was hard to sneak up and catch this spider, Dad, because most spiders have four pairs of eyes. That makes them able to see all around them," she said.

Edwina pointed to the front of its body. "Here are the spider's jaws. It crushes insects then sucks the soft insides into its mouth."

"Don't forget, Dad, very few spiders can hurt humans. Most spiders are more scared of us than we are of them!"

Web site

How do spiders build a web?

SPIDERS OFTEN begin a web by standing on a branch of tree or bush and spinning a read. They let the wind arry one end of the thread to other twig or branch. They alk across the thread and ild more of the web from e other side.

The spider keeps spinning y threads until it has built a me for the web. Then the ider begins to use a sticky k. It starts in the middle and es around and around wards the ends of the reads.

The best place to build a eb outside is near a light that on at night. Many insects around the light and get ught in the webs.

Did you know?

lost spiders can survive on nly one insect a day.

A spider's web is sticky to trap insects. It will stick to you too, if you touch one in the garden.

The crab war report

Tiny soldiers in culinary combat.

Dᴵᴰ ʏᴏᴜ ᴋɴᴏᴡ that crabs fight each other for food? Crabs always look ready for war. Their bodies, their four pairs of legs and their two **pincer** claws are covered in shell. This looks like **armour** and it works the same way too.

The shell is made of many pieces. It is jointed together so it can bend easily.

Crabs are very good at protecting themselves. They bury themselves in the wet sand if the tide is out so they cannot be seen by their enemies. This also protects them from the sun.

When a crab is fighting for its life it does not run away. The crab stands still with its pincer claws raised, ready to defend itself. The pincer claws are amazingly strong weapons. They hold on to things very tightly and are really sharp.

Did you know?

If a crab hurts his claw or gets it stuck, he can break the claw off at the joint and it will soon grow back. A crab can also re-grow its legs if necessary.

Hey, I've got my eye on you

And I'm hungry, too.

A CRAB'S EYES are on stalks. They are made up of hundreds of tiny eyes, so the crab can see whatever is happening all around it.

If a crab is in a fight, it pulls the stalks back into its shell to protect its eyes.

Between the crab's eyes are two pairs of antennae which circle around. Crabs use these to taste and smell.

Hairs all over the crab's body feel any movement in the water which warns the crab when danger is close by.

Crabs eat fish and worms. Parts of the shell over the mouth open and shut to tear the food as it is eaten. Inside the mouth, the food is quickly shredded until it is as fine as cotton wool. Hairs around the mouth sift out unwanted bits.

The crab uses its long, jointed legs to dig for food under sand. Its pincer claws catch and hold the food.

A garden of grasshoppers

Let's take a look up close.

A grasshopper has a long body which is protected by a hard shell.

WHEN YOU WALK through the garden on a warm summer night the air is full of buzzing and chirping noises. Some of those noises are made by grasshoppers.

These insects can be found where the weather is warm. They make sounds by rubbing their legs against their wings.

Grasshoppers live on the ground, in bushes, and in trees. If a grasshopper senses danger, it takes huge leaps using its powerful back legs.

Grasshoppers have large eyes, two short antennae, two pairs of wings and six legs. Even though it has wings a grasshopper rarely flies.

Grasshoppers eat plants. Their mouths have two pairs of jaws. The front pair bite, tear and chew the food. The other pair push the food down the throat. Both pairs of jaws move sideways rather than up and down.

Did you know?

A grasshopper cannot drink because its mouth can only bite and chew.

Beasty belly laughs

To tickle your funny bone.

Minibeast trivia

Minibeasts are all around
Some live above, some underground
Creatures can be large or small
Some may be short, while others tall
Some buzz, some hum, some croak, some sing
From tiny mites to bees that sting
Some are mooshy, others firm
Often they pass on a germ
Some minibeasts are born as eggs
Others have no wings or legs
Some carry homes upon their backs
Others leave dirty, smelly tracks
Some travel around with their brothers
Or hunt and trap and eat up others
A few have legs covered in hair
Some catch their food while in the air
When you see one don't be stressed
Sit back and watch and be impressed
They have so many skills, it's true
I wish I could do what they can do!

a poem by Minnie Critter

Who would believe that minibeasts could build a home this big? Team work and a lot of termites did it!

Editorial

Letters
to the editor

HOW many times have you heard someone frustrated shout "don't bug me!"? The word "bug" is often used in a negative way because people think that minibeasts are annoying.

We get sick of shooing away flies, and dodging bees and wasps. People don't like creepy, crawling spiders and smelly, dirty cockroaches. They are afraid of the germs mosquitoes carry.

Few people think about the good that minibeasts do. We would not have many of the fruits and vegetables we enjoy if it were not for minibeasts pollinating flowers. They make honey, destroy farm pests and are food for larger creatures.

Sometimes these minibeasts seem a bit yucky or scary, but the truth is we need them to exist because they help us to survive! They may be tiny, but they are very important!

Dear Editor,
Our neighbours have a big flowering tree that hangs over the fence into our garden and attracts bees in summer. This is a problem for us because we get many unwanted bees buzzing around our children when they are outside. We have asked our neighbours to deal with the problem many times, but they refuse.

Love BETTY, THE BEE BRIGADE

Dear Editor,
We have a holiday house in the country. It doesn't seem to matter how clean we leave it, because whenever we go back there, the kitchen benches are covered with smelly, oily trails left by cockroaches. I am sick and tired of it. The government should do something about those bugs.

Love CLEAN COLIN

Dear Editor,
We all have many bugs livin in our houses and gardens an most of the time we do no even realise that they ar there. Why do people ki insects or bugs that are n dangerous? If they do no want them in the house the should catch them and p them outside. There is no nee for them to die.

From CONCERNED CAROLINE

Lots of people kill spiders wheneve they see them, even though most spiders are harmless.

Ask Doctor Barry,
the bug expert

Dear Barry,
When we go out at night we leave the front door light on. The problem is that by the time we get home there are moths flying around our front door. Why are moths attracted to the light?

From IAN, THE INSECT INVESTIGATOR

BARRY: One explanation for this is that many moths use the moon to navigate at night. They sometimes confuse the lights with the moon and forget which direction to travel. They end up flying around and round in circles.

Dear Barry,
I really love butterflies. What is the best way for me to catch one to watch it more closely?

Love BOB, THE
BUTTERFLY BOY

BARRY: Butterflies are hard to catch. It is easier to catch a caterpillar and raise it to become a butterfly. When the butterfly hatches out you can observe it and then let it go.

Dear Barry,
My father says if you see one ant, you can be sure there are many others close by. Why do ants always travel in packs?

Love WANDA, THE
WASP WATCHER

*BARRY: Ants, bees and wasps are all social insects because they live in large groups. Each ant has a specialised job in its **colony** and if an ant was removed from its **community,** it would surely die.*

Watch out for wasps, they will sting you if you get too close.

Further resources

BOOKS

If you want to learn more about minibeasts, your school and local library are sure to have good books about them.

You might look for the Minibeast Pets series published by Wayland. Also try *Insects* or *Butterflies & Moths* or *Amazing Bugs* published by Dorling Kindersley.

Another good book is Paul Wright & Robert Pickett *Minibeasts* published by A & C Black.

These caterpillars will turn into butterflies.

CD-ROMS

Minibeasts and How They Live
Zoom into the amazing microscopic world of insects and other minibeasts with this interactive CD-ROM. From slitherers to wrigglers, this interactive multimedia package is full of facts, sounds, animations and much more.
Multimedia Bugs: the Complete Interactive Guide to Insects
Multimedia Bugs shows over 600 insects, including butterflies and moths, ants, spiders and many more. Special features, such as the creepy Slime Show and the exotic "Bugs that look like other things" section add entertainment value to the disc.
CD-ROM published by Inroads Interactive

NEWSPAPERS

Metropolitan newspapers may not be the best place to find information on minibeasts. You might find country newspapers have more information on minibeasts.

TELEVISION

Search for nature documentaries. These will often have information about insects and spiders.

VIDEOS & FILM

Animals Hear in Many Ways rev. ed.
A video that shows anima hear when their own bodie vibrate.
Animals that Build
This film focuses on all an mals who build to prote themselves.
Minibeasts
This video shows the grow of four animals—ladybir butterfly, spider and locust.

INTERNET

If you are interested in chec ing out sites and learnin more about minibeasts, have look at this site:
http://www.onthenet.com.a ~marna/minibeasts.htm
Click on the insect you wi to see. Ants, bees, butterfli etc. There are links to ma minibeasts from this site!

Glossary

BDOMEN—(say *ab-doh-en*) the part of a body that has the stomach. In insects nd spiders the abdomen is e last part of the body.
NTENNAE—(say *an-ten-*) feelers attached to the ead on some minibeasts.
PHID—(say *ay-fid*) a very ny insect.
RMOUR—a covering or ell that protects an imal.
OLONY—a group of osely related insects that e together.
OMMUNITY—a oup of animals or sects living and owing together in the me area.
RONE—a male honey bee. ones mate with young eens.
NVIRONMENT—the area d conditions where an ect lives.
CARGOT—(say *es-car-*) a snail that is eaten by ople.
ASTROPOD—(say *gas-h-pod*) an animal, such as nail, that has one muscular ot on which it glides about.
TCH—when a young mal comes out of an egg.

MATE—a partner to make babies with.
MOULTING—when old skin comes off because it has become too small.
PINCER—a pair of front claws.
POLLEN—a yellow grain-like substance in male flowers used to fertilise female flowers.

PUPA—(say *pew-pa*) a stage in the life of a baby insect before it becomes an adult.
THORAX—(say *thor-aks*) the chest, or middle part of an insect's body.

You'll never find an ant as big as this one!

Index

JOKES

Q. Where do spiders go to learn new words?
A. The WEBsters Dictionary.

Q. What's spiral in shape and very crowded?
A. A snail with a house guest.

Q. How do you start a lightning bug race?
A. On your marks, get set, glow.

Q. What do you get when you cross two insects and a rabbit?
A. Bugs Bunny.

Q. What is the best year for grasshoppers?
A. A leap year.

Earthworms are good for the garden and they make good fish bait too!